Read & Respond

FOR KS1

Read & Respond

FOR KS1

Author: Louise Carruthers

Editor: Vicky Butt

Development Editor: Simret Brar

Assistant Editor: Margaret Eaton

Series Designer: Anna Oliwa

Designer: Anna Oliwa

Cover Image: Jill Murphy

Illustrations: Jill Murphy, Gaynor Berry

Text © Louise Carruthers © 2008 Scholastic Ltd

Designed using Adobe InDesign

Published by Scholastic Ltd, Villiers House,
Clarendon Avenue, Leamington Spa,
Warwickshire CV32 5PR

www.scholastic.co.uk

Printed by Bell & Bain

1 2 3 4 5 6 7 8 9   8 9 0 1 2 3 4 5 6 7

British Library Cataloguing-in-Publication Data
A catalogue record for this book is available from the British
Library.

ISBN 978-1407-10042-5

Acknowledgements
Walker Books for the use of extracts and illustrations from
Five Minutes' Peace by Jill Murphy © 1986, Jill Murphy (1986,
Walker Books).

Five Minutes' Peace

About the book

Five Minutes' Peace is a delightful picture book about a family of warm-hearted elephants. The simple, engaging text is complemented by bright, colourful illustrations on every page.

Mrs Large wants five minutes' peace from her rowdy children so she sneaks upstairs to take a relaxing bath. Her peace is short lived. No sooner has she settled down in the bathtub with a tray of her favourite breakfast when one by one her three children come bursting into the bathroom. Grudgingly, Mrs Large listens to Lester play his recorder, Laura read her reading book and even lets the little one put his toys in the bath. But when the children pile into the bath with her, Mrs Large decides she has had enough. She goes downstairs where she has exactly three minutes and forty-five seconds of peace before the three children come and join her in the kitchen.

Five Minutes' Peace is an example of a story with a familiar setting. The simple plot centres on the relationships between the main characters. Young children will be able to draw on their own experiences of family life when exploring themes and issues raised by the text.

Five Minutes' Peace is an ideal text for use in the Key Stage 1 Literacy Hour. Shared reading of the story provides a context for teaching and applying word level skills and for developing children's understanding of sentence construction and punctuation. Children's understanding of character and dialogue can be developed through drama and role-play activities linked to the text.

The story is also an ideal stimulus for a wide range of creative writing activities.

About the author

Jill Murphy was born on 5 July 1949. She grew up in London where she attended the Ursuline Convent in Wimbledon. She later went on to study at Chelsea, Croydon and Camberwell Schools of Art. She worked in a children's home and as a nanny before becoming a freelance writer and illustrator.

Jill Murphy began writing her first novel, *The Worst Witch*, when she was 15. This title was the first in a series of books about an enthusiastic young witch, Mildred Hubble, who is the worst student at Miss Cackle's Academy for Witches. According to Murphy, the Worst Witch books are based on her own experiences at the convent where she was educated. *The Worst Witch* was made into a film in 1986.

Jill Murphy has written and illustrated many popular children's books since *The Worst Witch* was published in 1974. Her first picture book, *Peace at Last*, was commended for the Kate Greenaway Medal. She is well known for her bestselling picture books about the Large family, a caring but chaotic family of elephants. Titles in this series include *Five Minutes' Peace, All in One Piece, A Quiet Night In* and *Mr Large in Charge*. The Large family also features in a new CBeebies animation based on Jill Murphy's books.

Facts and figures

Five Minutes' Peace was first published in 1986 by Walker Books. It won the 1987 Best Books for Babies Award and was short-listed for the 1986 Children's Book Award. Other titles by Jill Murphy include *On the Way Home, Whatever Next?* and *The Last Noo Noo* (winner of the Smarties Book Prize 1995).

Guided reading

Introducing the book

Introduce the shared text. Use the title, cover pages, pictures and blurb to make predictions about the story.

Together with the children, look at the illustration on the front cover of the book. Pose a range of simple questions: *Who do you think are the main characters in the story? What are the elephants doing? What are they wearing? Do elephants really wear clothes and take bubble baths? Do you think this book is a fiction or non-fiction text? Why? Where do you think the story will take place? What do you think will happen?*

Help the children to identify and read the title of the story. Discuss the children's responses to the following questions: *What does the word 'peace' mean? Have you ever heard anyone use the phrase 'five minutes' peace'? Who do you think might want five minutes' peace in this story? Why?*

Read Jill Murphy's name on the front cover. Talk about who she is. Use the terms 'author' and 'illustrator'. Ask: *Do you know any other books Jill Murphy has written?*

Turn to the back cover and read the blurb to get a taste of the story. After reading the blurb, encourage the children to make predictions about what might happen in the story.

First reading

The first reading of the shared text is primarily for enjoyment. Read the story at a brisk, expressive pace, encouraging the children to join in as they feel confident. Emphasise directionality and one-to-one correspondence between spoken and written words by following the text with a pointer. Pause from time to time to ask children to predict a word/phrase or to speculate what might happen next in the story. For example: *Where do you think Mrs Large is going with her breakfast tray? Do you think the children will follow her into the bathroom?*

During the initial reading of the story, allow time for the children's spontaneous reaction and comments to the text and illustrations. Encourage the children to spend time exploring the humorous illustrations that enhance the text and bring the story to life.

After reading the text for the first time, ask some simple, targeted questions relating to the story to assess the children's understanding of the text. For example: *Why did Mrs Large tell the children to stay downstairs? Why did Laura say 'You like him better than me. It's not fair.'?*

Encourage the children to make links between the story and their personal experiences of wanting to be alone. Ask questions such as: *Have you ever wanted five minutes' peace? Where would you go to get five minutes' peace from someone in your family?*

Discuss the children's opinions of the book. Ask: *Did you like the story? Which part did you like best? Is there anything that you didn't like about the book?*

Encourage the children to explain *why* they liked/disliked particular aspects of the book.

Subsequent readings

In the first reading of the text it is vital that the enjoyment of the text remains paramount in the reading and exploration, and that the meaning is not lost. Subsequent readings of the text should be carefully planned to extend the children's comprehension of the text, build confidence and fluency when reading aloud and to provide opportunities for teaching and applying specific word and sentence level objectives. The children should be taught:

● how to use a range of decoding strategies to read unfamiliar words, check for meaning and to self-correct errors;

● to learn about word building and spelling patterns in context;

● to read, on sight, high frequency words;

● to develop understanding of sentence construction and punctuation;

● to read aloud with pace and expression appropriate to the grammar of the text;

● how to track the text from left to right and word by word;

● to understand and use correctly terms about books and print;

Guided reading

- about story elements (plot, character, setting);
- to predict and infer;
- to sequence the events of a story.

Story opening

Read the story up to 'That's why', stopping at some words to discuss the strategies used to read them, such as phonic knowledge, picture cues and re-reading sentences.

Discuss the story setting. Pose some simple questions: *Where does this story take place? What time of day is it? How do you know? What are the Large family having for breakfast?*

Encourage the children to consider why Mrs Large puts her breakfast on a tray and leaves the room. *Why doesn't she want to sit at the breakfast table with the children?* (It is very messy. The children are making a lot of noise.) Identify the phrase on page 1 that describes the scene. ('This was not a pleasant sight.') Ask the children to suggest other phrases that could be used to describe the scene at the breakfast table. (It was a terrible sight. It was an awful mess.)

Highlight the adverb on page 2 which describes how Mrs Large is leaving the room. ('sneaked'.) Ask: *Why is she trying to sneak out of the room without the children noticing?* (She wants five minutes' peace.) Encourage the children to suggest suitable alternatives for the word 'sneaked'. (Tiptoed, crept.)

On the stairs

Turn to the page in the book which begins 'Can *we* come?'. Ask the children to suggest why Lester, Laura and the baby are following Mrs Large upstairs. Encourage them to predict what Mrs Large might be saying. (For example: *Go back downstairs. Leave me alone, I need five minutes' peace.*)

Read the text with the children. Emphasise reading aloud with appropriate expression. Draw attention to devices that indicate how the text should be read, including speech marks, vocabulary (for example, 'muttered'), italics and question marks.

Underline the opening question: 'Can *we* come?'. Highlight the question mark. Ask: *What is special about this sentence? How do you know it is a question? Which words indicate who asked this question?* ('asked Lester'.) Identify and read the other question on this page. Model how to raise the intonation of your voice when reading a question aloud.

Five minutes' peace?

Continue reading the book, up to 'It was heaven'. Look at the illustration which depicts Mrs Large relaxing in the bath with a cup of tea. Ask the children to suggest words and phrases to describe how Mrs Large is feeling at this moment in the story. (Relaxed, happy, carefree.) Ask the children to find a phrase in the text that supports their view. ('It was heaven.') Brainstorm other phrases that could be used to describe the scene. (It was wonderful. It was so peaceful.)

Read on to the end of the next page. Notice how Lester manages to talk Mrs Large into letting him play his tune for her. Consider how Mrs Large feels now. (Annoyed, irritated.) Draw attention to significant words and phrases in the text. ('Must you?', 'sighed'.)

Turn to the next page and read on to 'Mrs Large groaned'. Ask the children to explain in their own words how Laura manages to persuade her mum to let her read her reading book. Have the children ever used a similar argument with their parents? Ask questions such as: *Why did Mrs Large say 'Thank you, dear' when the little one flung his toys into the bath water? Do you think she really wanted the toys in the bath with her?*

Reflect on the children's behaviour. Why don't they leave Mrs Large in peace? Discuss how Mrs Large might be feeling at this point in the story. (Fed up, annoyed.) Ask the children to imagine themselves in Mrs Large's situation. *Do you think you would have been so patient? How might you have behaved differently?* (For example: Told the children to go away and leave you alone. Sent the children downstairs to tidy up their mess.) Encourage the children to predict what might happen next in the story.

Guided reading

Enough's enough!

Turn to the next page in the book. Speculate about how Mrs Large is feeling now. (Angry, cross.) What is she thinking? Ask the children to put themselves in Mrs Large's position: *If you need some peace and quiet and someone came and disturbed you, how would it make you feel?* Before turning the page, ask the children to predict what happens next.

Read on to the end of the story with appropriate expression. Emphasise a raised voice at the end of each question. Discuss the story ending. Ask: *Do you think Mrs Large was expecting the children to come and join her? What do you think might happen next?*

Book review

Discuss the children's personal responses to the story and the characters. Ask: *Did you like the story? Who was your favourite character? Why? Which part of the story did you like best? Was there anything you did not like about this book?*

Encourage the children to empathise with Mrs Large's predicament at different points in the story by reflecting on their own experiences of wanting to be left alone. Tell them to imagine that they need five minutes' peace. Ask: *Where would you go? How would you feel if someone in your family came and disturbed you? Do you think you would stay calm like Mrs Large or would you behave differently?*

Shared reading

Extract 1

Use sticky notes to conceal the words 'breakfast', 'tray', 'plate', 'paper' and 'sneaked' on an enlarged copy of Extract 1.

Read the text together. Encourage the children to use a range of strategies to predict the missing words (for example, picture cues, grammatical knowledge and re-reading sentences). Reveal the concealed words and read the completed extract together.

Ask the children to describe the chaotic scene at the breakfast table. Identify the sentence in the text which sums up the mayhem. ("This was not a pleasant sight.') Invite the children to suggest other simple phrases that could be used to describe the scene.

Ask the children to name all of the things that Mrs Large put on her breakfast tray. Underline each of the items on the shared extract. Investigate the use of commas to separate each of the items in the list. Brainstorm a list of five different items that Mrs Large might put on her breakfast tray. Write the items in a sentence on the board. Challenge the children to insert commas in the correct places.

Extract 2

Together with the class, read an enlarged copy of Extract 2. Encourage the children to use a range of reading strategies to work out and check the meanings of unfamiliar words, such as using phonological, contextual and grammatical knowledge.

Talk about the purpose of speech marks. Underline all of the direct speech in the extract. Use a different colour for each character. Look for clues in the extract which show how the dialogue should be read. (Italicised text, question marks, vocabulary.)

Underline the word 'muttered' on the text extract. Consider how this word has been used to indicate exactly how the preceding dialogue should be read. Work together to add other words to the text to show how the children think the characters would be speaking. For example: 'No,' said Mrs Large **crossly**, 'you can't.' 'Because I want five minutes' peace from *you* lot,' **moaned** Mrs Large.

Divide the class into four groups. Re-read the extract, with each group reading the dialogue spoken by a different character.

Extract 3

Look at an enlarged copy of Extract 3. Ask the children to circle the full stops, speech marks, question marks and exclamation marks on the text extract. Discuss how the different forms of sentence punctuation influence how the text should be read. Talk about why some of the words have been written in italicised print. (For emphasis.)

Read the extract together with pace and expression appropriate to the grammar, punctuation and presentation of the text.

Underline all of the questions contained in the text extract. Identify which character is asking each question. Encourage the children to notice what the question sentences have in common. (They all start with the words 'Can I...' and end with a question mark.) Consider the responses Mrs Large gives to the children's questions. What do they tell us about how she is feeling?

Brainstorm other 'Can I...' questions that the children in the story might have asked Mrs Large. Write some of the children's suggestions on the board. Invite different children to draw a question mark at the end of each sentence.

Extract 1

The children were having breakfast.
This was not a pleasant sight.

Mrs Large took a tray from the cupboard.
She set it with a teapot, a milk jug, her
favourite cup and saucer, a plate of
marmalade toast and a leftover cake
from yesterday. She stuffed the morning
paper into her pocket and sneaked off
towards the door.

Illustration © 1986, Jill Murphy

Extract 2

"Where are you going with that tray,
Mum?" asked Laura.
"To the bathroom," said Mrs Large.
"Why?" asked the other two children.
"Because I want five minutes' peace
from *you* lot," said Mrs Large.
"That's why."

"Can *we* come?" asked Lester as they trailed
up the stairs behind her.
"No," said Mrs Large, "you can't."
"What shall *we* do then?" asked Laura.
"You can play," said Mrs Large. "Downstairs.
By yourselves. And keep an eye on the baby."
"I'm *not* a baby," muttered the little one.

Illustration © 1986, Jill Murphy

Extract 3

In came Laura. "Can I read you a page from my reading book? she asked.

"No, Laura," said Mrs Large. "Go on, *all* of you, off downstairs."

"You let Lester play his tune," said Laura.

"I heard. You like him better than me. It's not fair."

"Oh, don't be silly, Laura," said Mrs Large.

"Go *on* then. Just *one* page."

So Laura read. She read four and a half pages of "Little Red Riding Hood".

In came the little one with a trunkful of toys.

"For *you*!" he beamed, flinging them all into the bath water.

"Thank you, dear," said Mrs Large weakly.

"Can I have the cartoons in the paper?" asked Laura.

"Can I have the cake?" asked Lester.

"Can I get in with you?" asked the little one.

Mrs Large groaned.

Illustration © 1986, Jill Murphy

Plot, character and setting

In the spotlight

Objective: To explore familiar themes and characters through improvisation and role play.
You will need: *Five Minutes' Peace*, a spotlight or torch, a copy of photocopiable page 15 for each child.
Cross-curricular links: Drama

What to do
● After you have read the story with the class, choose four children to come to the front and make a freeze-frame (still picture) of the elephants having breakfast.
● Dim the lights. Shine the torch/spotlight on the child who is pretending to be Mrs Large. Ask the children to imagine how Mrs Large is feeling and what she might be thinking or saying at this point in the story. Choose several children to verbalise their ideas. (For example: 'Take that bowl off your head this instant!' or 'I can't stand this, I'm going upstairs for some peace and quiet!')

● Shine the spotlight on each of the other characters in turn and invite different children to suggest what they might be saying or thinking. Encourage the children to speak with appropriate intonation and expression. (For example: a cross voice for Mrs Large, a squeaky excited voice for the baby.)
● Make a series of freeze-frames to represent the main incidents in the story as illustrated in the shared text. Select different children to illustrate what the characters are doing in each scene.
● Hand out copies of photocopiable page 15. Ask the children to record one of their ideas in each speech bubble.

Differentiation
For older/more confident children: Ask the children to begin to use speech marks in their writing.
For younger/less confident children: Choose different children to sit in the 'hot seat' and pretend to be the main characters in the story.

Alternative ending

Objective: To compose a short, simple text by writing an alternative ending for a story.
You will need: Copies of *Five Minutes' Peace*, A4-sized paper, writing materials.

What to do
● Read the story with the children, pausing at different points to discuss the characters, setting and events.
● Focus on the story ending. Ask: *What happened at the end of the story? How many minutes' peace did Mrs Large have before the children came to join her in the kitchen? Did you like the ending? Why/why not? Did you predict the ending correctly the first time you heard the story?*
● Invite the children to share ideas for an alternative ending to the story. In shared writing, demonstrate how to rewrite and illustrate the final page in the book using one of the children's

suggestions. (For example: And off she went downstairs, where ....she had two minutes thirty seconds peace until the telephone rang; ...she had five minutes wonderful peace until the children came in and said sorry for making such a mess.)
● Give out paper and writing materials. Ask the children to write and illustrate a different ending for the story.
● Let each child read out their story ending to the rest of the group. Invite the class to vote for their favourite alternative ending.
● Re-read *Five Minutes' Peace* with the new ending which received the most votes.

Differentiation
For older/more confident children: Ask the children to adapt the story in other ways. (For example, set the story at bedtime.)
For younger/less confident children: Ask children to predict story endings from unfinished extracts.

Plot, character and setting

Not a pleasant sight!

Objective: To draw on knowledge of a text in deciding and planning what to write.
You will need: Copies of *Five Minutes' Peace*, writing materials.
Cross-curricular links: PSHE

What to do
● Look at the illustration on the first page of *Five Minutes' Peace*. Discuss the story setting together. Ask a variety of simple questions: *Where does this story take place? What time of day do you think it is? What are the Large family doing?*
● Read the text with the children. Consider what the author means by 'It was not a pleasant sight'.
● Tell the children to imagine they are 'in' the picture. Ask them to describe what they can see and the sounds they can hear.
● Encourage the use of imaginative and varied language, including a range of simple prepositions and interesting adjectives. (For example: There is a shiny blue toy car on the bench. There is a pool of sticky honey on the kitchen floor.)
● Build up a description of the story setting on the board using some of the children's ideas. Model how to rehearse sentences orally before writing them down. Demonstrate how to re-read the text to check for possible improvements or errors.
● Ask the children to write a piece of continuous prose to describe the story setting.

Differentiation
For older/more confident children: Encourage the children to write a description of the Large family's bathroom, based on the illustrations in *Five Minutes' Peace*.
For younger/less confident children: Ask the children to annotate a picture of the story setting with a short descriptive caption.

Change the story

Objective: To consider how different settings in a story can influence events and behaviour.
You will need: *Five Minutes' Peace*, photocopiable page 16, writing materials.

What to do
● Read the shared text together. Talk about the story setting. Ask the children to name the two rooms in the Large family home that feature in the story. (Kitchen, bathroom.) Discuss how specific events in the story are directly linked to the story setting.
● Ask the children to suggest other places within the primary story setting where Mrs Large could have gone to in order to find some peace and quiet. Compile a list of the children's suggestions on the board. (Her bedroom, the garden, etc.)
● Encourage the children to consider how the main events in the story might have been different if Jill Murphy had decided to set the middle part of the story in one of these places instead of the bathroom. For example, Mrs Large goes to her bedroom and has breakfast in bed. The children come and jump on the bed. Mrs Large goes to the living room and settles down to read her book. The children come in and argue about what to watch on the television.
● Hand out copies of photocopiable page 16 for the children to complete individually or in pairs.
● Talk to the children about their work. Ensure that the ideas they are writing about are relevant to the picture they have drawn.

Differentiation
For older/more confident children: Let the children write and illustrate an alternative version of *Five Minutes' Peace*. Ask them to use the ideas recorded on their photocopiable sheet to change the middle part of the story.
For younger/less confident children: Fill in photocopiable page 16 as a guided writing activity.

Plot, character and setting

Mrs Large

> **Objective:** To make adventurous word and language choices when building a character profile.
> **You will need:** *Five Minutes' Peace*, photocopiable page 17 (a copy for each child and one enlarged version), writing materials.

What to do

● Ask the children to name each of the characters in the story. What is their relationship to one another? (Mother, son/brother, daughter/sister.)

● Encourage the children to suggest words and phrases to describe Mrs Large in terms of her appearance. Write some of their suggestions in the first column of the table on the enlarged copy of photocopiable page 17.

● Ask the children, in pairs, to brainstorm words and phrases that describe Mrs Large in terms of her behaviour and qualities. (Kind, patient, tired, hardworking.) Let each pair feed back one of their ideas to the rest of the group. They should refer to the text to support their comments and opinions. (For example, Mrs Large is patient because she didn't get cross with the children when they kept disturbing her.) Record some of the children's suggestions in the second column of the table on the photocopiable sheet.

● Finally, use some of the children's ideas to model how to build up a simple character profile of Mrs Large.

● Give each child their own copy of photocopiable page 17 to complete.

> **Differentiation**
> **For older/more confident children:** Ask the children to write a simple character profile to describe one of the other characters in the story.
> **For younger/less confident children:** Repeat the activity for other characters from stories the children know well.

Three minutes and forty-five seconds of peace

> **Objective:** To explore familiar themes and characters through improvisation and role play.
> **You will need:** Copies of *Five Minutes' Peace*.
> **Cross-curricular links:** Drama

What to do

● Split the class into four groups. Allocate each group to play the part of one of the characters in the story. Read the narrative. Ask each group to read the dialogue spoken by their character with appropriate expression.

● Talk about the story. Ask: *Did Mrs Large get five minutes' peace? What happened when she went to the bathroom? Where did she go next? How many minutes' peace did Mrs Large get before the children came and joined her in the kitchen?*

● Working in groups of three, ask the children to speculate about what Laura, Lester and the baby might have been doing during the three minutes forty-five seconds that Mrs Large was in the kitchen by herself. (For example: The children got out of the bath, dried themselves and tidied the bathroom. / They ran about upstairs leaving wet footprints everywhere.) Spend several minutes working with each group. Ensure that the ideas the children are developing are relevant to the story setting and plot.

● Ask each group to devise a simple role play to show what the elephant children might have been doing before they went back downstairs.

● Watch and evaluate each group's role play.

> **Differentiation**
> **For older/more confident children:** Encourage the children to write their role play as a simple playscript.
> **For younger/less confident children:** Ask the children to underline the direct speech, using a different colour for each character.

Plot, character and setting

A peaceful place

> **Objective:** To create short simple texts that combine words with images.
> **You will need:** *Five Minutes' Peace*, pictures or photographs of peaceful settings (from the internet, Sunday supplements, travel brochures and so on).

What to do

● Discuss the story with the children. Ask: *Why did Mrs Large find it impossible to find five minutes' peace? Think about your own home. Who or what might disturb you in the bedroom or kitchen?*

● Ask the children to close their eyes and imagine a place that is very peaceful. Ask: *What is it about the place that makes it so peaceful? What can you see? What can you hear?* Encourage them to describe their 'peaceful place' to a partner.

● Next, show the children one of the 'peaceful setting' pictures. Ask them to help you compile a list of words that describe what the place is like. (Calm, still, quiet, wonderful and so on.) Turn some of their ideas into simple descriptive sentences. Draft a piece of shared writing that 'paints a picture' of the setting.

● Organise the children to work in pairs. Give each pair one of the 'peaceful setting' pictures. Ask them to look at the picture and imagine how it would feel to be in this place. Then, working individually or in pairs, ask the children to write a description of their 'peaceful setting' picture as modelled in the shared writing activity.

> **Differentiation**
> **For older/more confident children:** Show the children how to use a simple thesaurus to encourage the use of descriptive varied vocabulary.
> **For younger/less confident children:** Let the children take it in turns to describe one of the pictures orally. Ask the rest of the group to listen carefully and guess which of the peaceful settings they are describing.

Mapping the story

> **Objective:** To use planning to establish clear sections for writing.
> **You will need:** *Five Minutes' Peace*, writing materials, copies of photocopiable page 18 (enlarged to A3 size).

What to do

● Re-read the book with the class. Write the question 'What happened?' on the board. Ask the children to help you make a list of the key events in the story to represent the story plot.

● Explain that in this lesson you are going to show the children how to represent the story plot pictorially in the form of a story map which includes information about the main incidents in the story and where they take place.

● Organise the children so that they are sitting in a circle around an enlarged copy of photocopiable page 18. Ask a series of prompting questions such as: *Where did the story start? What could I draw/write to represent the kitchen and the events that took place there? What happened next?* (The elephants went upstairs.) *How could I show this on the story map?*

● Continue until each part of the story plot is represented. Annotate the story map with arrows to ensure that the order of events is clear.

● Retell the story using the information recorded on the story map.

● Finally, organise the children into small groups. Give each group an enlarged copy of photocopiable page 18. Encourage the groups to work together to illustrate and annotate a map of the story. Then invite them to retell the story in their own words.

> **Differentiation**
> **For older/more confident children:** Encourage the children to add extra details to their story maps (for example, speech bubbles).
> **For younger/less confident children:** Act as a scribe to help the children to record their ideas.

In the spotlight

- Look carefully at the pictures below. Imagine what each elephant is saying.
- Write a sentence in each of the speech bubbles to show what the elephants are saying.

Illustration © 1986, Jill Murphy

Plot, character and setting

Change the story

● Draw a different place where Mrs Large could have gone to get five minutes' peace.

[drawing box]

● Write about what might have happened there.

_____

_____

_____

_____

Plot, character and setting

SECTION
4

Mrs Large

- Think of some words and phrases that describe what Mrs Large looks like and what sort of character she is.
- Write the words in the table below.

Appearance	Character

- Now use some of your ideas to write a character profile for Mrs Large.
- Remember to write in sentences.

_____

_____

_____

_____

_____

Mapping the story

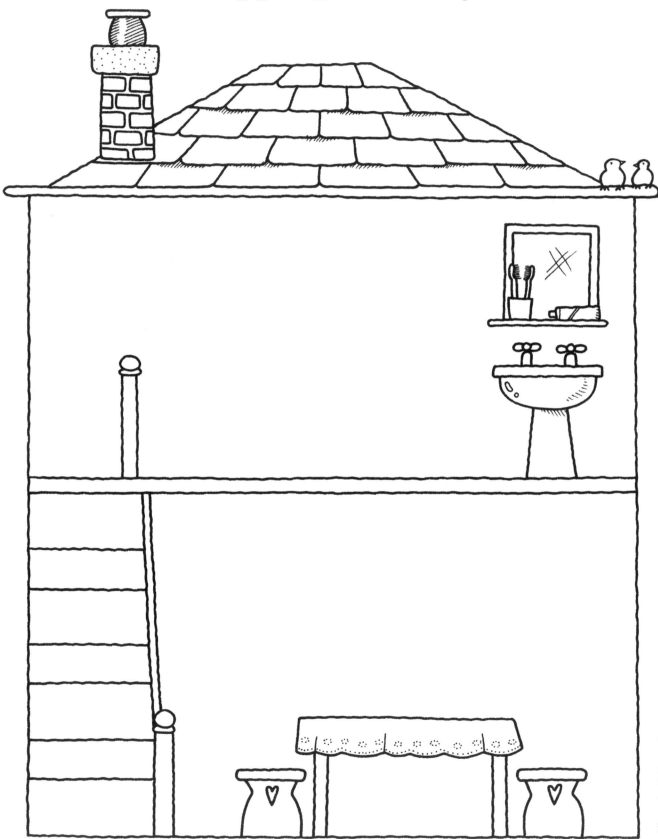

Illustration © Gaynor Berry

Talk about it

Leave me alone

Objective: To comment on events, characters and ideas, making imaginative links to their own experiences.
You will need: *Five Minutes' Peace*, copies of photocopiable page 22, writing materials.

What to do
● Read the story opening together. Encourage the children to describe the chaotic scene at the breakfast table. Ask: *Why do you think Mrs Large doesn't want to sit at the table with the children to eat her breakfast? Why doesn't she want the children to follow her upstairs? Why does she want to be left alone? How is she feeling?*
● Encourage each child to tell the group about an occasion when they wanted to be left alone. Ask them to describe why they wanted to be left alone, how they felt and where they went. (For example: 'One day at school some big children were teasing me in the playground. I felt upset and so I went to sit on the bench.')
● After each child has recounted their experience, invite the rest of the group to ask relevant questions to find out more detail about the experiences that they have heard.
● Hand out copies of photocopiable page 22 for each child to complete. Instruct the children to draw an appropriate picture in each box and then complete the sentences below.
● Ask each child to share their completed piece of work with a partner.

Differentiation
For older/more confident children: Ask the children to write a detailed recount of an occasion when they wanted to be left alone.
For younger/less confident children: In a shared writing activity, ask the children to fill in photocopiable page 22 from Mrs Large's perspective.

Role plays

Objective: To explore familiar themes and characters through role play.
You will need: *Five Minutes' Peace*, a set of plot cards from photocopiable page 23.
Cross-curricular links: Drama

What to do
● Re-read the story with the class. Discuss why Mrs Large wanted to be left alone. Ask the children to suggest other reasons why a person might wish to be left alone. (For example: if they are feeling sad, embarrassed, tired, angry, annoyed, upset.)
● Organise the children to work in groups of three or four. Explain that you would like each group to plan and perform a simple role play about someone who wants to be left alone. Give each group one of the cards from photocopiable page 23. Ask them to devise a short role play based on the information on the card.
● For example, Card 1 requires the children to act out a simple scenario set within the home environment in which something happens to make the main character feel angry and want to be alone. (For example: James is naughty. His Mum tells him that he is not allowed to watch his favourite television programme and so he goes up to his room in a bad mood.) Allow sufficient time for the children to prepare and rehearse their performances.
● Let each group perform their role play. Invite the rest of the class to say what they like about each performance and to make suggestions for improvement.

Differentiation
For older/more confident children: Ask the children to write a simple playscript based on the role play they have presented to the group.
For younger/less confident children: Support the children in the role-play activity.

Talk about it

On the telephone

Objective: To act out a well-known story, using voices for characters.
You will need: *Five Minutes' Peace*, two toy telephones/mobile phones, simple character props (for example, a tie for Mr Large, newspaper and rollers for Mrs Large), a picture of Mr Large, a table and chair.
Cross-curricular links: Drama

What to do

● Before the lesson, draw a picture of Mr Large. Show it to the children. Ask: *Who is this? What is his relationship to the other characters in the story?* (Father, husband.) Speculate why Mr Large does not feature in the story. Ask: *Where do you think he might have been?* (Prompt suggestions such as at work, in bed, washing the car.)
● Choose a volunteer to pretend to be Mrs Large sitting at the kitchen table reading her newspaper (as illustrated at the end of *Five Minutes' Peace*).
● Put on a tie and assume the role of Mr Large (at work). Using vocal expression appropriate to the character, announce: *I think I will just give Mrs Large a ring to see if she is having a good morning.*
● Have a conversation in character. Ask simple prompt questions to encourage Mrs Large to recount the events of the morning: *What are you doing? Are the children behaving themselves? What did you have for your breakfast?* Offer sympathy or advice as appropriate.
● Organise the children to work in pairs. Ask them to pretend that they are Mr and Mrs Large having a telephone conversation about the morning's events.
● Choose volunteers to perform their dialogue to the rest of the group.

Differentiation
For older/more confident children: Encourage the children to write a recount of Mrs Large's busy morning.
For younger/less confident children: Invite the children to brainstorm a list of questions that Mr Large might ask Mrs Large.

A good start to the day

Objective: To answer questions, make relevant contributions and take turns to speak.
You will need: Pictures, photos or real examples of breakfast foods and drinks (a selection of cereal packets, fruit, toast, various spreads, eggs), A3-sized paper, writing materials.
Cross-curricular links: Science, PSHE

What to do

● Invite each child to describe what they like to eat and drink for breakfast.
● Use the illustrations in *Five Minutes' Peace* to help the children recall all the different foods that the Large family ate for breakfast. Ask: *Have you ever had a cake for breakfast? Do you think eating cake is a healthy way to start the day?* (Remember to be sensitive to individual circumstances.)
● Talk about why breakfast is considered to be an important meal. Look at a selection of breakfast foods and drinks (see 'You will need'). If possible, allow the children the opportunity to taste some of the foods and drinks (be aware of any food allergies beforehand). Ask them to explain which of the foods they consider healthy and which they consider unhealthy. Why?
● Organise the children to work in groups of two or three. Ask them to work together to make a poster which promotes the importance of eating a healthy breakfast.

Differentiation
For older/more confident children: Organise the children into small groups. Ask them to make a short presentation about the importance of eating a healthy breakfast.
For younger/less confident children: Ask the children to draw and label a picture of their favourite breakfast foods.

Talk about it

Hardworking mum

> **Objective:** To tell stories and describe incidents from their own experience.
> **You will need:** Copies of *Five Minutes' Peace*, writing materials.
> **Cross-curricular links:** PSHE

What to do
● Talk about the role of Mrs Large in the story. Pose the following questions: *Why do you think Mrs Large needed five minutes' peace? Do you think she has had a busy morning? What do you think she has been doing?* (Making breakfast, getting the children out of bed and so on.)
● Encourage the children to talk about how their own mothers help them. (For example: making the breakfast, taking them to school, giving them a cuddle when they feel sad.) Remember to be sensitive to individual children's circumstances. For some children, it may be necessary to substitute a different family member or carer. Alternatively, you may wish to simply let the children talk about a family member of their choice.
● Ask each child to write and illustrate a page for a shared book about the sorts of things their mums (or families) do to help them.
● Bind the children's work together to make a book. Working collectively, make a front and back cover and agree on a suitable title.

> **Differentiation**
> **For older/more confident children:** Discuss how the children could thank their mums for all that they do for them.
> **For younger/less confident children:** Play a miming game. Invite pairs of children to mime different things that their mums do for them. Encourage the rest of the group to guess what action the children are miming.

My special place

> **Objective:** To take turns to speak; to visualise events, making links to their own experiences.
> **You will need:** *Five Minutes' Peace*, a 'speaking object', photocopiable page 24, pencils.
> **Cross-curricular links:** PSHE/Citizenship

What to do
● Read up to 'muttered the little one'. Discuss the text and accompanying illustrations. Ask questions such as: *Where is Mrs Large going? Why doesn't she want the children to follow her?* Establish that Mrs Large is going to the bathroom because she wants to have some quiet time away from the children. Consider why she has chosen the bathroom over other rooms in the house.
● Pass a 'speaking object' around the circle. Ask each child to finish the following sentence when it is their turn to speak: *When I want to be alone I go to…* (For example: …my bedroom to play with my toys, …the garden and sit on the swing.) Encourage the children to explain why they have named a particular location. (For example: It is quiet. I can lock the door.)
● Read on to the end of the story. Use information from the text and illustrations to infer how Mrs Large feels when the children follow her into the bathroom. (Annoyed, cross.) Encourage the children to empathise with Mrs Large by asking them to describe how they would feel if someone intruded on them in their special place.
● Finally, provide each child with a copy of photocopiable page 24 and ask them to complete it independently.

> **Differentiation**
> **For older/more confident children:** Ask the children to write a detailed description of the special place where they go when they want to be alone.
> **For younger/less confident children:** Encourage the children to draw and label a picture of their special place.

Talk about it

Leave me alone

I wanted to be on my own because

_____

_____

_____

I felt _____

_____

_____

_____

I went to _____

_____

_____

_____

Role plays

Setting: Home **Characters**: Family **Feeling**: Angry	**Setting**: Home **Characters**: Family **Feeling**: Annoyed
Setting: School **Characters**: Teacher **Feeling**: Upset	**Setting**: School **Characters**: Friends **Feeling**: Embarrassed
Setting: Park **Characters**: Friends **Feeling**: Upset	**Setting**: School **Characters**: Friends **Feeling**: Angry

Talk about it

My special place

Mrs Large went upstairs to the bathroom to try and get five minutes' peace.

● Draw a picture of the place in your home that you would go to if you wanted to be alone.

● Write about how you would feel if somebody came into your special place and disturbed you.

_____

_____

_____

_____

_____

Get writing

Non-fiction books

> **Objective:** To create short simple texts that combine words with images.
> **You will need:** *Five Minutes' Peace*, non-fiction books about elephants, writing materials.
> **Cross-curricular links:** Science

What to do

● Ask the children: *Do elephants live in houses? Do elephants eat cornflakes? Is this a fiction or a non-fiction book? How do you know?*

● Tell the children that you would like them to make a simple non-fiction book about elephants which contains factual information about where elephants live and what types of food they eat.

● Share a non-fiction book about elephants. Model how to use the contents page (or index) to locate relevant information. Record facts in note form under the headings 'Where do elephants live?' and 'What do elephants eat?'.

● Working in pairs/small groups, ask the children to use the non-fiction books to find out other facts about elephants (habitat and feeding).

● Invite the children to write and illustrate a simple non-fiction book about elephants, using the questions on the board as page headings. Encourage them to use some of the key features of non-fiction texts (pictures, captions, subheadings, labelled diagrams and so on).

● Ask the children make a front cover and contents page for their book.

> **Differentiation**
> **For older/more confident children:** Ask the children to research other information about elephants to make additional pages for their books.
> **For younger/less confident children:** Encourage the children to write a caption for a page in a shared book about elephants.

Book review

> **Objective:** To maintain consistency in non-narrative, including purpose and tense.
> **You will need:** Copies of *Five Minutes' Peace*, photocopiable page 28 (one enlarged copy and copies for each child), writing materials.

What to do

● Read and discuss the story. Focus on the children's views of the book. Throughout the discussion, encourage them to explain why they like/dislike different aspects of the book.

● Discuss the children's opinions of the layout of the book, how the text is presented and the quality of the illustrations.

● Invite the children to express personal responses to the story. *Did you enjoy the story? Who was your favourite character? Why? Is there anything that you don't like about this book? How could the book be improved?* (For example: humorous speech bubbles, a different title.)

● Display an enlarged copy of the writing frame on photocopiable page 28. Read the sentence openings. Ask the children to suggest how the story plot can be summarised in a few sentences. Invite different children to say how they would complete the remaining sentence openings, giving justification for their opinions. (For example: *My favourite character is the baby because he is just like my brother.*) Encourage the children to use the joining word 'because' to link sentences.

● Hand out copies of photocopiable page 28. Ask each child to complete the sentence openings to write a personal review of *Five Minutes' Peace*.

> **Differentiation**
> **For older/more confident children:** Ask the children to write an extended review of another book that they have studied.
> **For younger/less confident children:** Invite the children to draw and label a picture of their favourite character in the story.

READ & RESPOND: Activities based on *Five Minutes' Peace*

Get writing

Labels

> **Objective:** To write labels for drawings and diagrams.
> **You will need:** A non-fiction book or poster containing examples of labelled pictures and diagrams, photocopiable page 29 (one enlarged copy and copies for each child), writing materials.
> **Cross-curricular links:** Science

What to do

● Look at several examples of labelled pictures and diagrams. Discuss the purpose of labels. (To identify and name significant parts of an object or picture.)

● Look at an enlarged copy of photocopiable page 29. Ask the children to name the items on the tray. Explain that you would like them to help you label each of these items.

● Look at the key words in the box. Encourage the children to use their phonic knowledge to help them to read the words.

● Choose a child to write a label for one of the items on the tray. Demonstrate how to draw a line to join the label to the appropriate part of the picture. Talk about the purpose of this line. (It shows the reader precisely which part of the picture the label corresponds to.)

● Choose different children to label the remaining items on the breakfast tray.

● Hand out photocopiable page 29 for the children to complete independently.

> **Differentiation**
> **For older/more confident children:** Ask the children to label illustrations in the shared text. Encourage them to apply their phonological knowledge to have a go at spelling unfamiliar words.
> **For younger/less confident children:** Set a breakfast tray using real objects. Make a small label for each object on the tray. Let the children practise labelling the items correctly.

Where is it?

> **Objectives:** To use capital letters and full stops when punctuating simple sentences; to use simple prepositions to describe the position of objects.
> **You will need:** *Five Minutes' Peace*, writing materials.
> **Cross-curricular links:** Mathematics

What to do

● Look at the illustration on the first page of *Five Minutes' Peace*. Ask: *Where is the teddy?* Encourage the children to answer in a complete sentence. (For example: The teddy is next to the cup. The teddy is on the bench between the car and the cup.)

● Write one of the children's responses as a sentence on the board. Encourage the children to use their phonological knowledge and sight vocabulary to spell words. Demonstrate how to demarcate the sentence with a capital letter and a full stop.

● Re-read the sentence. Identify and underline the word in the sentence that describes the position of the teddy.

● Pose other simple 'where' questions about the illustration: *Where is the spoon? Where is the picture?* Write the answers on the board. Highlight the preposition in each sentence.

● Ask the children to write a list of simple sentences that describe the position of different objects in the Large family kitchen. Remind them to include a preposition in each sentence and to demarcate each sentence with a capital letter and full stop.

> **Differentiation**
> **For older/more confident children:** Encourage the children to modify the noun in each sentence with a simple adjective. For example: 'The *fluffy* teddy is next to the *red* cup.'
> **For younger/less confident children:** Ask the children to choose the correct preposition from a word bank to complete simple sentences.

Get writing

Marmalade toast

> **Objective:** To write simple instructions.
> **You will need:** Bread, toaster, plate, knife, butter, marmalade, photocopiable page 30 (one enlarged copy and copies for each child), writing materials.

What to do

● Let the children share their own experiences of breakfast time. Ask: *What do you like to eat? Who makes your breakfast?*

● Recall which character in *Five Minutes' Peace* had marmalade toast for breakfast. Make some marmalade toast. Invite different children to help with each step of the process.

● Look at an enlarged copy of the writing frame on photocopiable page 30. Ask the children to identify what type of text it is. Consider why people use recipes. Explain that a recipe is an example of an instructional text because it describes how to do something.

● Read the headings on the photocopiable sheet. Discuss the purpose of each section and clarify the meaning of any unfamiliar vocabulary.

● Remind the class of key features of instruction texts (short, concise sentences written in the imperative; numbered steps, each beginning on a new line, and so on).

● Invite the children to write a recipe for marmalade toast, using the writing frame provided on photocopiable page 30.

● In a subsequent lesson, let the children follow and evaluate their own instructions.

> **Differentiation**
> **For older/more confident children:** Ask children to use words such as *first, next* and *finally* to emphasise the chronological sequence of the instructions.
> **For younger/less confident children:** Ask the children to draw a sequence of pictures that demonstrates each step in the recipe.

Questions

> **Objectives:** To compose simple sentences; to use question marks.
> **You will need:** *Five Minutes' Peace*, writing materials, plastic overlay sheet and a dry-wipe pen.

What to do

● Read from 'Where are you going with that tray, Mum?' to 'muttered the little one'. Model reading with pace and expression appropriate to the grammar (pause after each full stop/comma, use a raised voice for questions).

● Using a plastic overlay sheet and a dry-wipe pen, underline the first line of text. Circle the question mark. Ask: *What is special about this sentence? How do you know it is a question? Who asked this question? How do you know?*

● Talk briefly about why people ask questions. (For example, to seek permission/help or to ask for information.) Look for other examples of questions being asked in the story. Focus the children's attention on the type of words that are used at the beginning of the question sentences. Compile a list of these words on the board along with others that the children are able to suggest (where, can, what, who, when, have, and so on).

● Ask the children to think of questions that they might ask (or be asked) in their home environment. Write several of their ideas on the board. Emphasise the question mark at the end of each sentence by writing it in a different colour.

● Hand out paper and pencils and ask the children to write their own list of questions.

● Invite different children to read out their list of questions using appropriate expression.

> **Differentiation**
> **For older/more confident children:** Ask the children to write a suitable response to each question.
> **For younger/less confident children:** Let the children record their questions on a tape recorder.

Book review

Title _____

Publisher _____

Author _____

Illustrator _____

This story is about _____

_____

_____

My favourite character is _____

because _____

_____

My favourite line from the book is _____

_____

_____

My favourite part of the story is _____

_____

_____

Labels

● Use the words in the box below to label each of the items on the breakfast tray.

| bowl | orange juice | apple | spoon | box of cereal | jug of milk |

● On the back of this sheet draw a picture of the things you would choose to put on your special breakfast tray. Label each of the items.
● Remember to draw a line to join each label to the correct part of the picture.

Illustration © Gaynor Berry

How to make marmalade toast

Ingredients:

_____

_____

_____

_____

_____

Equipment:

_____

_____

_____

_____

What to do:

1 _____

_____

_____

_____

_____

_____

_____

_____

_____

Assessment

Assessment advice

Ongoing formative assessment of children's achievements and progress in literacy is essential. It allows teachers to make judgements about the progress that individuals are making towards achieving specific learning targets and to ensure that future learning activities are planned at an appropriate level. Outcomes of assessments can enable teachers to set new targets for each child. Reporting and teacher assessment need to be based on evidence, which should be drawn from a child's practical work and from classroom discussion.

Formative assessment for learning may take a variety of forms, including observations, discussion and questioning, analysis of children's work and peer- or self-assessment. Children's performance in all of the activities in this book

can be evaluated using one or more of these assessment techniques.

Each of the activities in this book has a clear, assessable learning objective which states what it is aimed that children should know/be able to do by the end of the lesson. In order to involve children fully in their learning, teachers should share these learning goals with the children at the beginning of each activity.

At the end of an activity it is important to reflect back to the learning target to help the children understand what they have done well and where they will go next with their learning.

The assessment activity on photocopiable page 32 can be used as part of a record of individual children's progress. It provides a framework for assessing children's story writing ability.

Story plan

> **Assessment focus:** To draw on knowledge and experience of texts in deciding and planning what and how to write.
> **You will need:** *Five Minutes' Peace*, photocopiable page 32 (one enlarged version and copies for each child), writing materials.

What to do

● Re-read *Five Minutes' Peace* with the children. Ask some simple questions to assess the children's understanding of the key story elements (plot, character, setting) in relation to this text. Ask: *Where does the story take place? Who is the main character? Why did Mrs Large need five minutes' peace? Where did she go? What happened?*

● On an enlarged copy of photocopiable page 32, use a shared writing session to complete the story planning frame for *Five Minutes' Peace*.

● Next, explain to the children that you would like them to write their own 'five minutes' peace' stories.

● Give each child a copy of photocopiable page 32 to complete a plan for a new story. Ask them to make notes about the story setting, characters and plot.

● Go around the class, talking to individual children about their work. Ask them to tell you what is going to happen in their story. Check that their story plots are appropriate to the story setting they have chosen.

● Once the children have finished writing their story plan on the photocopiable sheet, ask them to use it to write their own story about someone who wants five minutes' peace.

> **Differentiation**
> **For older/more confident children:** Encourage the children to add narrative and description, and to be adventurous with vocabulary.
> **For younger/less confident children:** Let the children make a storyboard to show the sequence of events in their story. Ask them to write a one-sentence caption below each picture to describe what is happening.

Story plan

● Plan and write your own story about someone who wants five minutes' peace.

Title: Five Minutes' Peace

Main characters:

Setting:

What happens in the story?

Why does the main character need five minutes' peace?

Where do they go?

What happens next?

How does the story end?